HEřMANOVCE

FOUR SEASONS WITH THE ROMA

JARRET SCHECTER

EDITED BY FRANCESCA SORRENTI

Eerie, surreal, desperate—
these are the words that come
to mind after walking across
the rickety bridge to the
impoverished Roma settlement
that is separated from the rest
of Hermanovce by only two
small streams. Just beyond the
thin ribbons of water littered
with debris, a tranquil village
and picturesque countryside
are physically accessible,
yet elusive in every other way.
Being abandoned and stranded
amongst the surrounding
prosperity and beauty has
made the peninsula a ghetto
of melancholy and despair.

The mood described above also
creeps inside the homes of the
Roma. The sad structures are
usually composed of just one
or two cramped rooms, a
dilapidated ceiling, and many
mismatched and dirty carpets
strewn together. Exposed and
spliced wires usually lead to an
unadorned light bulb hanging
in the middle of the room and
sometimes to what is often
the most prized possession,
a television set. Frequently,
there are Christian icons on the
barren walls, a wood-burning
fireplace in the corner, and a
thin mattress that also plays
host to fleas and lice.

These are a people that have
been historically marginalized
for hundreds of years, and
the millions of Roma people
living across Europe continue
to suffer in extraordinary
ways. Unless radical
change takes place, these
disenfranchised citizens will
not benefit from Slovakia's
membership to the so-called
progressive European Union.
Technically, the neglect of
these men, women, and
children might not be a crime,
but it certainly is a sin
against humanity.

Jarret Schecter

VOZAR, 80, is the second husband of Vozarani. Originally, he was a blacksmith, like his father and grandfather, but later worked as a wagon driver and then as a tractor operator at the local agricultural cooperative. Like many Roma, he does not use his given name and instead goes by Vozar, which is Roma, as well as Slovak for "coachman." Despite being a generally quiet and unassuming man, he is quick to proudly present his old driver's license emphasizing that everybody needed him at one time. As proof of his popularity, Vozar has a collection of old televisions—at least 20 of them—in his small house. Most of the sets don't work, but he is proud of these gifts that his "white friends" have presented him.

Between the homes, there are **ALLEYS** leading to little squares that, for the better part of the year, are filled with either mud or snow. And even when they are packed with people going about their daily business, these common areas are empty and joyless places.

In the Hermanovce settlement,
as in most Roma communities,
roughly half of the inhabitants
are fifteen-years-old or younger.
The approximate age of females
giving birth for the first time
is just under seventeen, and
their fertility rates are much
higher than those among the
non-Roma **POPULATION**.
To outsiders, this has often been
perceived as a threat and a
demographic time bomb.

The communist government, at one time, tried to reduce the danger of a Roma population explosion by **STERILIZING** their women, arguing that families with fewer children will do better. The surgery was done usually after the women delivered a child in a maternity hospital. Some of the mothers agreed to the surgery before and, as a kind of compensation, accepted a certain amount of money which they usually used to improve the living conditions of their families. Some women, however, later claimed the surgery was done without their prior agreement or knowledge.

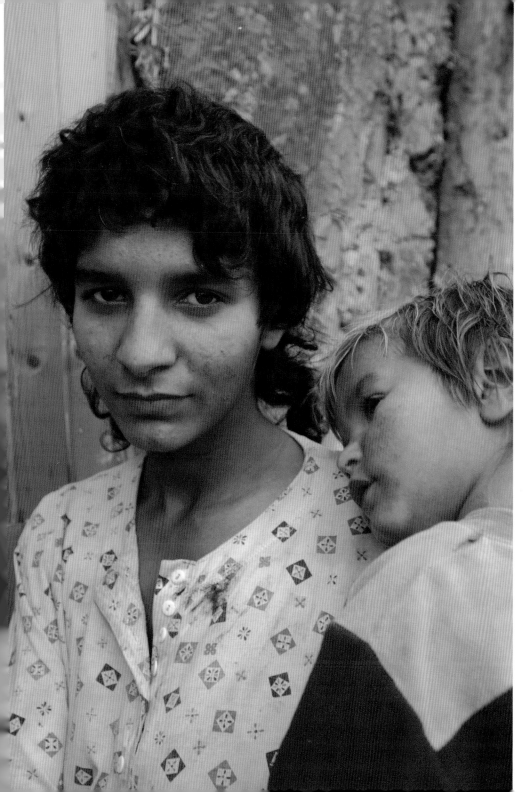

In summer, when it is too hot inside their small huts, the Roma prefer to not only sleep outdoors, but to cook there, as well. Most **TRADITIONAL** meals are based on carbohydrates and fat and are similar to traditional Slovak dishes. They include halushky or small boiled dumplings of mashed potatoes and wheat powder and marikli, a kind of flat bread baked on a stove or stone. The most interesting thing, however, is not the food itself, but the very strict guidelines connected to consumption and diet. At all costs, the Roma avoid eating "impure" meat, such as that from carcasses or dogs. And meals have to be prepared according to strict hygienic rules: it is forbidden to cook in a pot used for washing one's body or clothes.

JASHCHUR has no job and his wife is crippled by a stroke. They live from month to month on social welfare, much like everyone else in the settlement. Perhaps it is because of these reasons that Jashchur is one of the few older adults in the settlement who not only drinks cheap alcohol, but also inhales the fumes of paint thinner, an accessible and inexpensive drug of sorts. And while people here are not too judgmental about excessive drinking and smoking, and, in fact, often take great pleasure in doing so, the act of sniffing is considered extremely base behavior. As a result, Jashchur's status is very low in the settlement, and he is not welcome in even the homes of close relatives.

MANIA, 60, has "only" three children, all of whom have grown up and left the settlement. She is, however, raising the two small sons of her daughter. When the girl's first marriage broke up, the court decided that her mother should take care of the children. She also watches after her two grandsons and her husband, carefully cleaning their little house and cooking for them every day. "I cannot read very well, but I know how to cook," she says about herself proudly. This situation is not rare in the world of the Roma. Women often become mothers relatively early and, in many situations, the welfare system decides that it's best to entrust the children to older relations, usually the grandparents.

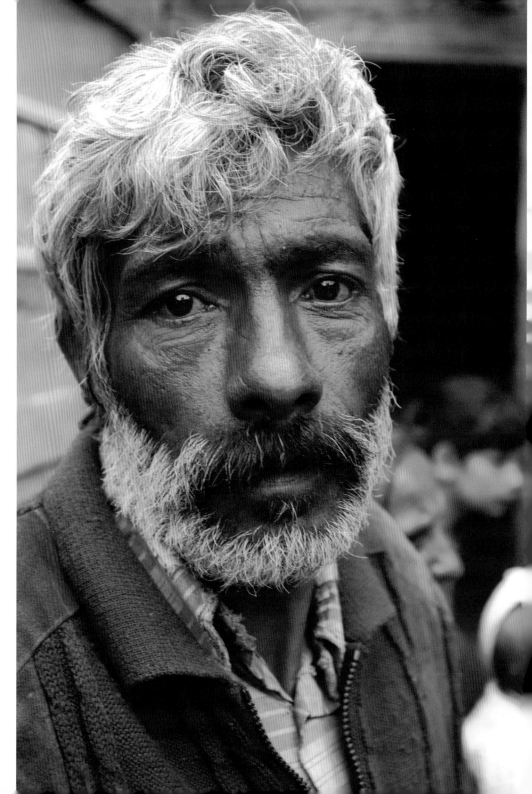

High birth rates among the Roma are a source of tension in the region. Non-Roma are potentially afraid of being outnumbered, and they perceive the Roma as having children in order to gain child **WELFARE** payments. While economic support of any kind is always welcome when there are financial constraints, people will always have babies whether or not they are supported by a welfare system. Children are simply the easiest source of joy in a world where there is little or plenty.

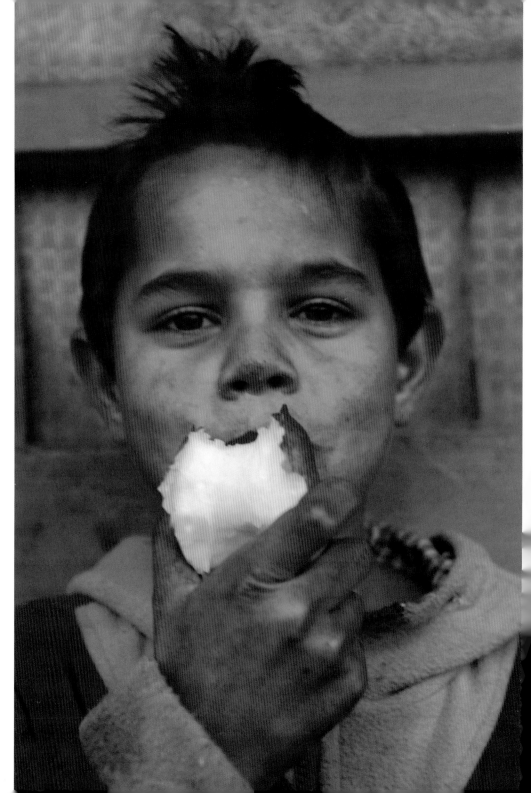

In the Hermanovce settlement, **VOZARANI**, 90, is the mother of seven, a grandmother ten times over. And great grandmother of literally everyone. In addition to her strong bloodline, Vozarani's other source of pride is her beauty. Even today it is easy to understand how beautiful she used to be when she was young—something she is not shy to remind any listener of. And if a person is too impatient to listen to her tales of the boys who admired her and cannot take the time to look beyond the lines on her face, Vozarani's red hair is an attempt to remind the world of how striking a girl she once was.

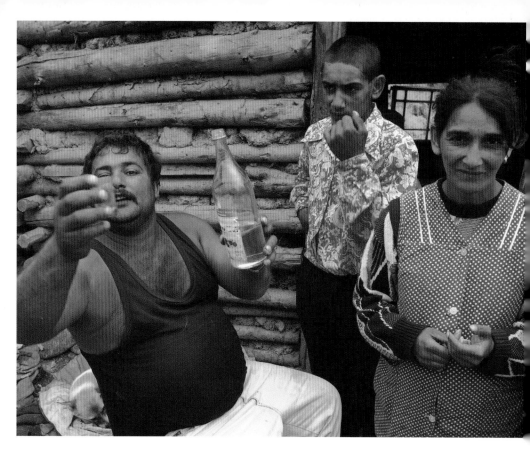

The Roma live in an extremely stratified society similar to the caste system of India. One can be perceived as a zuzo (pure) or as degesh (polluted). To not become polluted is one of the main practical and spiritual concerns in the life of every Roma. **PUPURKA**, the woman in the center, belongs to the less prestigious group, but when she was young, her beauty inspired a boy from the "better" caste to fall in love with her. Despite the protests of his family, the two moved in together. This resulted in the boy's mother beating Pupurka on several occasions and trying to drive the pair apart. In the end, she succeeded. Eventually, Pupurka married **ZABAK**, and the couple has raised ten children in this simple hut of wood insulated with clay and grass.

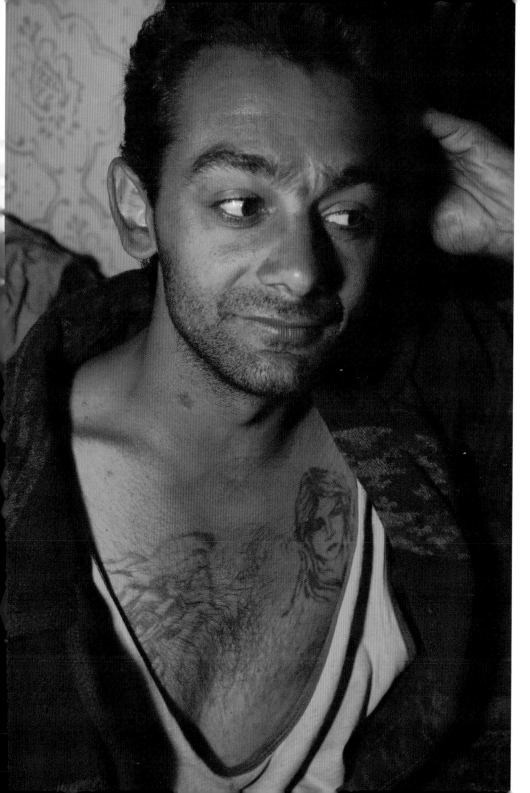

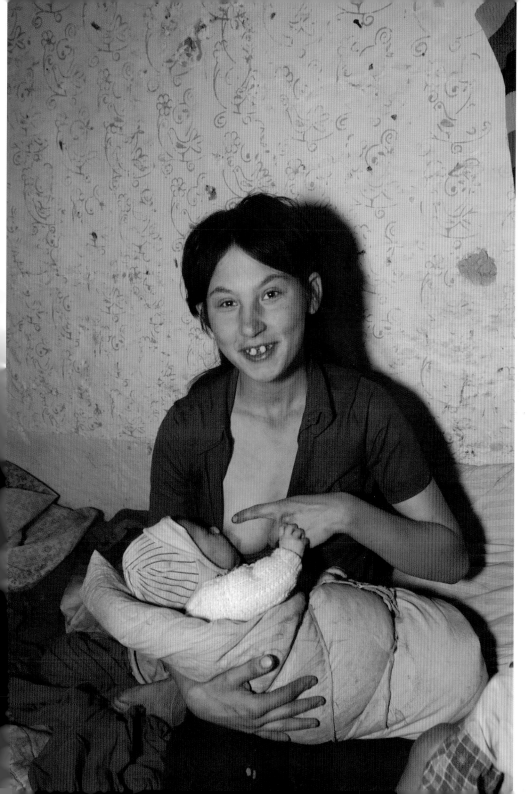

If a Roma family has an
IMPURE guest, they serve that
person food on special plates
or throw the dishes away
afterwards. They would never
use the dishes themselves
for they would then become
polluted as well. This custom
maintains a certain social
stratification, not unlike the
caste system in India where
the Roma came from originally.

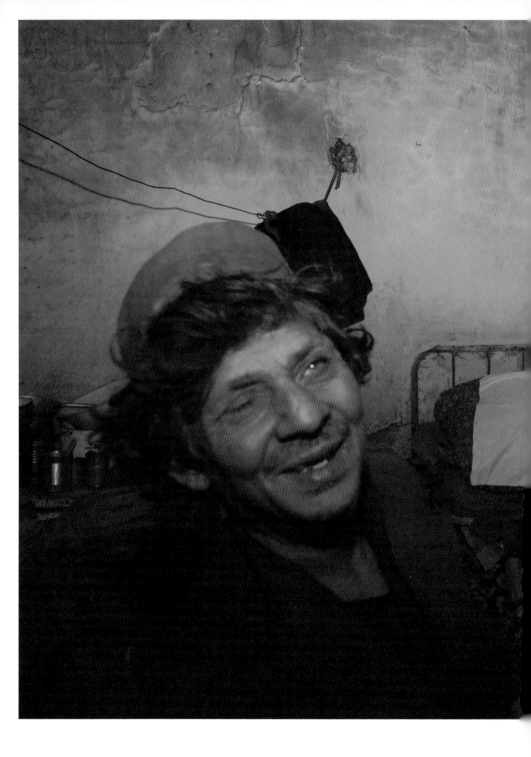

The Roma believe in a
SUPERNATURAL power that
transcends their existence—
something which they
conceptualize as God—but they
do not generally feel any need
to participate in regular
Christian services. They will
say that they are Christian if
you want to hear it and they
buy and display sacred pictures
and statues in their homes,
but they do not attend church.
In general, Roma need a priest
only for baptizing their young
and for burying their dead.
They believe that un-baptized
or improperly buried individuals
will come back as a "mulo,"
or ghost to potentially threaten
and harm its relatives.
Sometimes, this belief is
exploited by priests who
may refuse to baptize a baby
unless its parents get married
in the church.

The term **HUSBAND** is actually something of a misnomer, as the Roma do not generally feel the need to apply for official marriage registration. Men and women often choose instead to simply live together, sometimes for a lifetime like many traditional legally recognized unions. But because the state covers much of the cost of child welfare, women do not have to depend on their husbands financially, and "divorce" can be an easy affair. In many cases, old bonds are quickly replaced by new ones.

EMILKO is the son of Vozarani and Vozar, and despite being over forty, he still lives with his parents. This is an unusual situation for Roma culture, but it is only because he is somewhat mentally handicapped. Emilko is also blind in his right eye, and there are two stories as to why. In one version, he was doing construction work at the farm of a villager as a young man, and some unslaked lime accidentally fell into his eye, burning it. Another less spoken of account says that a taunting youth threw the lime on purpose. Most people in the settlement are reluctant to discuss what really happened, making it seem that the latter story and its lingering shame may well be the truth.

HISHKA, 57, was extremely
pretty when she was
young. Twenty years ago,
a photographer visited the
settlement and took a picture
of her and her little daughter.
She was so beautiful in the
photo that it was used for a
poster. A copy still hangs in a
privileged place in her house.
But her youth is gone now
and her health is getting worse,
as she never forgets to remind
a listener and then asks for
a cigarette. Hishka, like most
Roma, is a devoted and
passionate smoker. Despite the
consequences, she refuses to
quit under any circumstances.
Once she returned from
a hospital, not completely
cured of her pneumonia,
with a cigarette in her mouth.
In general, the lives of the
Roma are far from healthy.

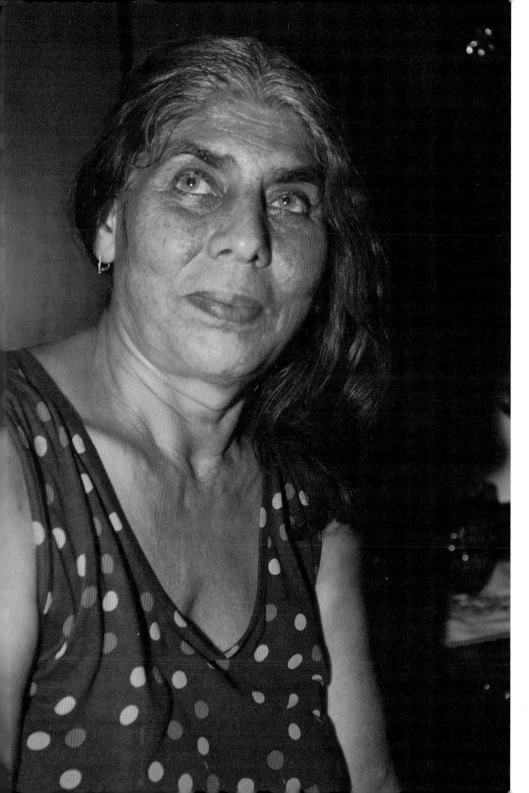

THE ROMA.

Roma, or Gypsies as they are known pejoratively to many, has historically been difficult and often filled with a certain amount of poverty and desperation.

A comparative study of the Roma language points to India as being their original homeland, but beginning in the 9th century, they migrated north with long stops in Persia, Asia Minor, and Greece. From the 12th century onwards, they proceeded more deeply into the territory of the Balkan Peninsula and Panonia lowlands, appearing in Central Europe in the 13th century. For a good part of the 14th century, the European population accepted the Roma, who had started calling themselves Christian pilgrims on their travels, but the situation eventually devolved. As the numbers of these wanderers increased and encroached on more economically developed areas, the attitudes of Europe changed. At that point, the Roma's skills in metalworking and music weren't as unique or needed. More and more, they were accused of robbery and other petty crimes, and soon they were branded parasitic outsiders. Shortly thereafter, they were accused of not only thievery, but of witchcraft, and the attitude of the surrounding society that had tolerated them with masked indignation before, turned to open hate.

With the excommunication of the Roma by the Archbishop of Paris in 1427, these hostile attitudes became officially sanctioned. In 1500, the Imperial Council of Maximilian I announced an edict in which the Roma were to leave the German nations as quickly as possible or face capital punishment. Billboards depicting the bodies of hanged Roma were displayed along the borders of the former kingdom of Bohemia as a warning to those who considered entering the country. This violent prejudice followed them into the 20th century, when about 500,000 European Roma perished in the concentration and work camps of World War II.

The Roma who lived in Slovakia might have mercifully escaped the genocide, but various discriminatory regulations at the time still affected their lives; they were not allowed to use public transportation; they could enter villages only on certain days and hours; and the men were forced into labor in special work camps. And if they were lucky, their settlements were moved to less desirable areas, away from the villages. Otherwise, their homes were often burned to the ground.

In the area of eastern Slovakia, where the Hermanovce settlement is located, the situation for the Roma was somewhat more favorable than in the western parts of Europe. The Roma were present there at least from the 14th century, performing jobs that weren't as attractive or profitable for the majority. They offered services

The long winding road to the eastern Slovakian village of Hermanovce runs along the upper part of a hillside offering a lush and romantic view of the Rivulet Hermanka and of the surrounding countryside. Coming around the last bend, a panorama unfurls of colorful roofs, topping scores of simple but attractive cottages. But a little further along, there's a peninsula formed by the rivulet measuring roughly 100 by 30 metres and containing around fifty ramshackle structures. It is this smaller subset of Hermanovce that houses a population of some 300 Roma. This settlement is not a matter of pride to its inhabitants or to the 1,200 non-Roma population living in proper houses higher up the stream. In fact, both communities feel deeply ashamed of it. The huts built from slim branches and clay mortar, and situated on dirt paths are an eyesore to the rest of the village. The Roma recognize that their place in the world is not unlike their physical environment: poor, neglected, muddy, defiant, and marginal. The life of the

not practiced by the local inhabitants including black-smithing, producing bricks, making wooden pots, and even fulfilling the role of musicians in the feudal courts.

The Roma settled in villages and towns primarily because there was a certain, albeit limited, demand for the work they could contribute. But eventually history repeated itself, and the local market could support only a limited number of people offering those specific skills and services. And owing to the general nature of population growth, it became very difficult to maintain groups with large numbers. As a result, regular segmentation occurred when one group stayed in the original locale and others split off to not-so-distant areas looking for more opportunities. The various parties would try to maintain contact, so when it was convenient, they could bring in an outside man or woman for purposes of marriage. This practice kept the Roma isolated not only from the majority of "native inhabitants," but also from other more distantly located Roma groups and populations of different ancestral origins.

The Hermanovce settlement evolved in this traditional way. Local registry records mention that in the 1880's, four brothers who lived in the periphery of the village Hermanovce (probably the descendants of the first settled Roma couple) married two pairs of sisters from a near-by village settlement. These brothers and their children were blacksmiths, and their descendants manufactured bricks and wooden troughs, and did seasonal agricultural work. The reward for these services was usually granted in kind, not in money—a bartering strategy that helped them survive on the edge of the majority society.

As the numbers of Roma in Hermanovce grew, however, the possibilities of a legitimate livelihood decreased and the conflicts and troubles between the two populations increased. Today, there are many cases of Roma stealing from the gardens, stores, and homes of non-Roma, but they suffer forms of unauthorized retaliation. It is not uncommon for policeman to break into Roma huts in the middle of the night looking for crime suspects and using physical force to coerce confessions that may or may not be true.

The reality, though, is that the Roma and the non-Roma are already competitors at the lowest rungs of the social scale. The unemployment rate within the settlement is 100%, and in the whole Hermanovce region, it is often up to 40%. Currently, the entire Roma population lives on social welfare, and with survival at stake, they have been forced to take on radical forms of subsistence. On the other side of the rivulet, their non-Roma neighbors fear losing what little they already have. In the end, both elements of society have become enmeshed in a vicious circle of hate and abuse: the Roma feel beggared and pushed aside and the non-Roma feel robbed and abused. In a way, both sides are right from their respective points of view, and both behave within the range of their cultural values.

It seems that the only escape from this cycle would be a massive economic development of the whole area, but even then, profound attempts would be needed to adjust the cultural values, attitudes, and behavior of both groups. It is a situation that money alone cannot solve.

One way or another, all the players in this drama are humans with emotions and motives in their actions. If we were unaware of the cultural logic behind their actions, it would be all too easy to disregard them. This book is an attempt to give the Roma of the Hermanovce settlement a face and voice.

Jaroslav Skupnik

A VERY SPECIAL THANKS:
I would like to thank Jaroslav
Skupnik for bringing reality to
my pictures through his
insightful writing. I would
like to thank my editor,
Francesca Sorrenti of Ske
group, for her encouragement
in creating this book with
inspiration and for applying
her knowledge to this project.
David Cashion for his editing.
And to Wai and Martin
for their creative design.
Not forgetting Gigi for
believing in me.

A SPECIAL THANKS TO: The
Roma people of Hermanovce
for their warmth, kindness,
and hospitality.

Vachla
Banik & Albina
Vajkus & Beta
Jokar & Irenka
Kacka & Arabela

THANKS TO:
Marvin & Marian
Darrow & Diana
Francis
Christine Lozier
Steve Sutton
Davide ske

Marisha & Hiro Shibuya
Kristyna Navratilova
Cathy Lang Ho
Seina Van Clark
Rowena Daly
Katie Meister
Marty Tillman
Dan Recht
Charles Harriman
Luca and Nicla
Andrew Lass
Harriet & Martin Ottenheimer
Frantisek Vrhel
Luca & Nicla
Sasa Musinka
Blanka Kufnerova
Klara Pravdova
Karel Novak
Martin Jazairi
Lida & Pavel Satrovi
Petr Kornacki
Ondra Novak
Jana Rybkova
Ivo Budil
David Scheffel
Frantisek Margita
Blanka Kufnerova
Sasa Musinka
Klara Pravdova
Karel Novak
Martin Jazairi
Lida & Pavel Satrovi
Petr Kornacki
Ondra Novak
Jana Rybkova

Published in Great Britain
in 2003 by Trolley Ltd Unit 5
Building 13, Long Street,
London E2 8HN, UK
Distributed by Phaidon Press

Photography © 2003
Jarret Schecter
Text © 2003 Jaroslav Skupnik
Editor: Francesca Sorrenti
Text Editing: David E. Cashion

10 9 8 7 6 5 4 3 2 1

A catalogue record for this
book is available from the
British Library

ISBN 0-9542648-7-8

Design by M&W @
Fruitmachine

Printed in Italy by Soso